CW01582399

I am a Shepherd

Alan Barwell

I AM A SHEPHERD

Copyright © Alan Barwell, 2015

ISBN-13: 978-1518794704
ISBN-10: 151879470X

The right of Alan Barwell to be identified as the author of this work has been asserted in accordance with the Copyright, Designs and Patents Acts 1988.

All rights reserved. No part of this publication may be reproduced, stored in a retrieval system, or transmitted in any form or by any means, electronic, mechanical, photocopying, recording or otherwise, without the prior permission of the publishers.

All images contained within this work are taken from the public domain.

I am a Shepherd
Contents

Story One

Joseph

My name is Joseph. I was born the son of Jacob. The first son of my mother, Rachel, but the eleventh son of my father. My father, Jacob, spoiled me because I was the son of his favourite wife. Sometime later I had another brother, he was called Benjamin. But, unfortunately, that came at the cost of the death of my mother who died at childbirth.

My father and his twin brother didn't always get along but they came together to bury my grandfather, Isaac. In the same way, my ten older brothers did not like me because I was my father's favourite. It made them mad! It made them mad when my father gave me a special coat. To explain why, let me tell you something about the coat.

The coat was like a best coat… the sort of coat you could do no work in. And, as my father wanted me to wear it all the time, this meant that I did hardly any work while the others worked hard looking after our sheep and goats.

Things got worse when God gave me a dream. We were all binding up sheaves of corn. Then, I saw their sheaves all bowing down to mine! I told them about this, and they said: "You think we are going to bow down to the ground! Ha! Who do you think you are?"

I had another dream, we were all stars. I was a star and they were all stars. And, their stars, and the sun and the moon, all bowed down to my star! I told my brothers and my father this dream too. My father rebuked me and said: "Shall I and your mother, and your brothers, all bow down before you?!"

I was more unpopular now than I ever was before, but I felt I had to tell them what I saw. My brothers didn't like it one bit. They didn't like it because I told my father about the bad things they did when they were out tending the sheep.

Then one day, my father said to me: "Your brothers have gone to Shechem to graze the sheep. I want you to go and see how they are getting on and come back here and tell me how the flocks are."

So, off I went and when I reached Shechem they were nowhere to be seen! Typical! But I saw was a man. He said that they had moved on to Dothan. So, off I went to find them.

When they saw me coming, the seemed to be talking about me. They grabbed me. They held me tight. They threw me in a pit. Some of them wanted to kill me! But Ruben, my eldest brother, stopped them. And so, they just left me there in a hole in the ground.

Sometime later, I heard them talking. They pulled me out of the pit, ripped off my coat and sold me to some travelling Ishmaelites for twenty pieces of silver.

These Ishmaelites were on their way to Egypt. So, now I was on my way to Egypt to be sold. I just did not know what to think. But, still I thought: God was with me.

* * *

When we got to Egypt, I was sold to a man called Potiphar. I worked hard and everything I did seemed to please my master. Very soon, I was in charge of the other servants and put in charge of just about everything in the house, the finance and all the business my master was involved with. Things just seemed to be going well; God was blessing me in all I was doing.

Then one day, my boss said he was going away on business and was leaving me in charge of everything. I felt so proud... but you know what they say pride comes before a fall. His wife thought she was free to take advantage of me. She tried to do all sorts of things to me. I just kept avoiding her. But one day, when I had to go into the house, she got hold of my robe. I struggled. I tried to get away, as I did she pulled it off me and I ran out!

When the boss came back she made out, in revenge, I had done terrible things to her. He was mad and had me thrown into prison even though I had done no wrong.

So, for the second time, I was treated badly - and yet I just couldn't see what I had done wrong! I still thought God was with me. In time, I showed the guard I was someone to be trusted and so I was allowed certain privileges. I became a helper and other prisoners were soon coming to me for help.

When I was in this prison, there was a bit of a stir and two of Pharaoh's servants were locked away too. After a day or two, they came to see me. They said they had been having dreams. They had heard that I understood dreams. Of course, I said that sometimes God shows me what dreams mean.

The butler came in and told me his dream. He said there were three vines and the grapes grew. He squeezed the grapes and put the wine in Pharaoh's cup. He was pleased. I knew what this one meant.

"In three days you will be back waiting on Pharaoh," I said.

He went away happy and so the baker came to me next. He said that his dream had been about three baskets of bread on his head. The birds swooped down and ate all the bread. Unfortunately, I knew what this one meant too.

"In three days, you will lose your head and will be killed," I replied.

It came to pass that the last thing I told the butler, before he left the jail, was to mention me before Pharaoh. But, he forgot about me and the years just kept rolling by. I trusted God but, I can tell you, being in prison could get depressing.

* * *

Then two years later, one day some soldiers came in and asked for me. They ordered me:

"You have to go and see Pharaoh!"

As you can imagine I was scared. Normally, when anyone had to go and see Pharaoh they were going to be put to death.

I was brought into the palace and dragged up in front of Pharaoh. He asked:

"Are you Joseph?"

I stammered my reply: "Y…y…yes."

"They tell me you have a gift with dreams. I've had dreams. I cannot rest until I find out what they mean. Will you help me?

"I will try to, sir," I said extremely nervously.

"Well," he said, "I dreamed and in my dream there were cows. There were seven fat cows; strong cows. There were also seven lean, skinny cows. Then suddenly, the seven skinny ones ate up the seven fat ones.

"I went back to sleep, but the dreaming didn't end there! I dreamt that seven stalks of wheat sprung up from the ground. They were full of corn. Then skinny stalks of wheat sprung up from the ground. The east wind blew and the skinny stalks ate the fat ones. Then I woke up in a sweat again!"

I prayed to God and asked Him what to say to Pharaoh. Then God told me what to say. I told Pharaoh that the seven fat cows and seven fat stalks meant that there would be seven years of very good harvests. Then the seven thin cows and dismal stalks of wheat meant that there would be seven years of famine.

I told him that he would have seven years to build up a stock of produce so that Egypt would have plenty when the famine came.

Pharaoh replied: "We must have a man that is wise and is understanding what God is doing. There is nobody better for the job than you, Joseph."

Pharaoh took the ring off his finger and put it on mine. He put a gold robe around me and gave me the second chariot of Egypt.

"I am Pharaoh in Egypt, you are next. No one is above you and no one can do anything without your word."

Pharaoh gave me a wife. So, here I was, second in command of Egypt at thirty years of age! From being in a pit then in a cell – to this!

* * *

The next seven years we built storehouse upon storehouse. We had to have enough food to last seven years. It was a job that took up all of my time. But living in the lap of luxury wasn't all that bad!

The drought came.

I knew that I had to control the amount of food that went out because we had to last seven years! Since the famine was not just in Egypt but all of the lands, people soon got to know that there was food in Egypt. And, if people came from other countries, I was the one who decided whether they should be given food and how much.

One day, my servant said that there were ten men from Canaan. He asked me how much to give them. I heard what he said. I just had this feeling. I went to see these men from Canaan…

It was my ten brothers. The ones that had sold me to become a slave. I did not speak to them directly. I talked to them by an interpreter, pretending not to understand them. They said they were all sons of one man.

"You are spies!" I said, "You have come to spy out the land."

They replied: "Lord, we are ten of twelve brothers. The youngest is at home with our aging father."

I said: "I want to see this other brother, then I will believe that you are not spies."

They talked amongst themselves. I could hear them say that this was their punishment for what they had done to Joseph. I could hear them say that this was their punishment for what they had done to me!

They just didn't understand that I knew what they were saying. They just didn't understand that I was their brother.

I left them worrying for three days, then I took Simeon and locked him up and sent the others home. In their sacks was the money that they had paid me. I knew they would be worried when they got home and would have to tell their father that they could not go again unless they also brought Benjamin back to Egypt.

The time seemed to drag. Would they come back? Would I be able to see my little brother again?

I left word that if they came back again, I was to be told straight away.

The day came. They brought money for the corn and the money they had found in their sacks when they got home. When they came, I told my servant to bring them to my house to eat.

They were frightened. They told the steward what had happened the first time with the money and that they had brought it back.

I sat them down in order of age. They were amazed. At that I had to leave the room a few times to weep. When they were there I said: "Is this the younger brother."

"Yes, my lord," they replied.

The next morning, we packed them off and put the money in their sacks again. But, I put my gold cup, in Benjamin's sack.

As soon as they were gone a little while, I sent my soldiers after them to accuse them of stealing my cup. The guards took Benjamin after finding the cup in his sack. When it was found, all the brothers came back. They weren't going back without him.

Judah came to me to offer himself in the place of his brother. I just couldn't keep up the pretence any longer. I sent all the Egyptians out of the room.

I said: "I am your brother, Joseph." They stood back in fear.

"Do not worry that you sold me," I continued, "it was all in God's plan. It was part of God's plan for me to save you when the famine swept the land."

I wept so loudly that they could hear me outside.

"Is my father still alive?" I asked.

"Yes," they said.

I told them that the famine had five more years to run and that they must bring him to Egypt so that I may take care of the whole family.

They left and reached home. My father did not believe them until he saw the wagons I sent to transport them back to Egypt.

I was reunited with my father. We all prospered in Egypt.

It is amazing how God looks after His people. It is amazing how my childhood dreams meant so much. It is amazing how God can turn bad situations out for the best.

Story Two

Moses

My name is Moses. I was brought up in a large Egyptian palace. I lived the life of a prince under the care of Pharaoh. In fact, Pharaoh's own daughter was the one I called 'mother.'

I was taught be some of the best teachers and was educated to a high standard. When I grew older, I was taught to fight and I was very fit. I acted like an Egyptian. I did all the things an Egyptian was meant to do. I even spoke like an Egyptian. But, deep down, I just knew I wasn't one of the Egyptians.

I was a Hebrew. I came from one of the tribes that were slaves in Egypt. I never really bothered about the slaves. In fact, I never hardly saw any of them. I knew that my real, Hebrew, blood-mother had nursed me and cared for me.

I just wasn't one of them.

As the years went by, I began to think about them more and more. I just couldn't get them out of my mind. So, one day I went to find out more.

As I walked, I saw an Egyptian hurting a Hebrew man. I stepped in. I tried to stop it. The Egyptian turned on me. But I was stronger… I had been trained to kill. Before the flash of an eye, I suddenly realised that I had killed him. Without thinking, I buried him in the sand.

Thinking that it was all over, I returned to the normal routine. The next day, I was walking along when I saw two

Hebrews fighting. I stepped in to try and stop them. I was completely taken aback when one said:

"Are you going to kill me like you killed the Egyptian yesterday?"

I was utterly shocked. I thought that no one knew! What if Pharaoh found out? What should I do?

I decided to run… I started out across the desert. I had no idea where I was going or even where I was. I just wanted to be as far away from Pharaoh as possible.

I went on mile after mile. There seemed to be no end to it. Tired. Thirsty. Hungry. I was almost at the stage of collapsing when, in the distance, I saw trees.

It was an oasis! Fruit to eat… water to drink! I ate and fell asleep in exhaustion.

Suddenly, I could hear the bleating of sheep. I was awoken by a family of girls drawing water for their sheep. Some men arrived and started to drive away the sheep. They were trying to take the water the girls had drawn in order to water their goats!

Using my soldier skills, I knew I could defeat the men. They were no match for me!

The girls were so grateful that they invited me to their camp where their father greeted me. He thanked me for protecting his girls. He explained that he only had girls and, as such, had no sons to look after the sheep. So, the girls had become his shepherds.

I stayed the night. And another night. I was invited to stay as long as I liked. So, I stayed helping to look after the sheep.

Over time, I fell in love. And so, I married the father's oldest daughter. Her name was Zipporah.

We had a son together. Life was good. I was at last settled.

But the story doesn't end there! One day, we moved the flocks near to what the people of the camp called the 'Mountain of God'. This was not an unusual thing to happen. But, I saw something odd. Something out of the ordinary.

I saw a tree on fire. But what was strange was although the flames were raging, the tree just didn't seem to be burning. I got closer and closer to get a better view.

"Moses..." came a whisper. The voice seemed like it was coming from the tree!

"Moses..." it repeated, "Take off your shoes, you are on holy ground."

Without even thinking, I took my shoes off. I was scared. I just didn't understand what was happening.

The voice then started to tell me about the plight of the Hebrews in Egypt. The voice said that he wanted me to go and tell Pharaoh to let the Hebrews go.

I thought: "You must be joking! Me? Go to Pharaoh? Come on... he's not going to take any notice of me! Anyway, who am I supposed to tell them has sent me?!"

"Tell them 'I am' has sent you."

"I can't talk to Pharaoh... I stutter..." I replied quickly, trying to find any excuse or way out of this.

"Your brother, Aaron, will help you. Now, take your rod and throw it on the ground."

I did just what the voice told me. I threw it down and it transformed into a snake. I jumped in fear and grabbed its tail. As I did, it turned back instantly into a rod.

"Do that in front of Pharaoh..."

* * *

So, in fear and trepidation, I went to find Aaron. We told the people and headed for the palace.

Pharaoh, as you can imagine, was not impressed when my rod turned into a snake. He told his magicians to do the same. But as they did, my snake ate theirs.

Pharaoh got mad and said the Hebrews now had to go and get their own straw to make bricks. I felt terrible. Things had got worse for the Hebrews... not better!

The next morning God sent me back to the palace. I told Pharaoh that they would have no water. I told him all the water would turn into blood. And just as I predicted, it happened. But still, he wouldn't listen.

Eight more times I went to Pharaoh pleading. I went each time and predicted a different plague every time. But still, he wouldn't listen.

There were flies, frogs, locust, hail, and fire. But, each time Pharaoh got more stubborn.

Then, came the worst of all. God frightened me. He told me that every first born child in Egypt would die. I told the people to put blood of the lintels of their doors so that the angel of death would pass over them. I told them to be ready to leave the next day.

We ate our meals, but that night was different to any other night I've lived through. Although we were safe, nobody had been through a night like that.

Daylight came. Pharaoh could not get rid of us fast enough. Two million Hebrews! I prayed to the Lord to help me. How was I meant to lead all of those people out of Egypt?

*   *   *

We started our journey, all seemed to be going well and we reached the Red Sea. We all set up camp for the night.

As we rose the next morning, we heard a noise like thunder. In the distance we saw Pharaoh's chariots coming. The people panicked. They shouted at me saying:

"You brought us here!"

"You've brought us out of Egypt to die!"

The Lord then put a pillar of fire between us and the Egyptians and told me to hold out my staff over the water.

As I did what He asked, the sea started to roar. It opened up and showed a pathway to safety. God said:

"Lead the people. Lead them across the dry ground."

It was amazing! We crossed the ground over the sea bed. I had never seen the like! But little did we know that this wasn't the end of the miracle!

God took the pillar of fire away. It was the only thing separating us from the Egyptians! They charged after us but as soon as the last Hebrew was on safe ground, God closed the sea over them.

We were all amazed. My sister Miriam led the people in singing.

We moved on to the 'Mountain of God.' I told the people I was going up to talk with God and seek His advice on what we were to do and where we were to go.

When I got up the mountain, the presence of the Lord was overwhelming. I stayed there many days, the Lord gave me 'Ten Commandments' written in stone for the Hebrews.

Time didn't mean anything, it was so fantastic. I just sat there in God's presence. Nothing else seemed to have any importance.

God turned to me and said: "Go down the mountain."

I could hear a lot of noise.

"It sounds like war," I replied.

"The people have turned to wicked ways. They are turning to worship idols."

When I reached the base of the mountain, I saw the people partying. They were worshiping a golden calf. When they saw me they were shocked. They say that my face glowed with light and I can only guess that it was the result of being with God for so long.

I destroyed the calf. And, the tablets of stone were smashed and broken in two.

Lots of the Hebrews stood by their idol. So, God caused an earthquake. Many people were killed. The rest swore allegiance to God.

I returned up the mountain. God wanted to destroy them all but I pleaded with Him to hold back His anger. Well, that was the first time I pleaded their case… and it wouldn't be the last.

We got to the border of the 'Promised Land'. I sent in spies to look at the land.

Eight out of the ten spies came back saying that there were giants in the land and that we could never defeat them.

Only Joshua and Caleb said we could go, defeat the foes and win the land. So, the people said that they wouldn't go. Because of their lack of belief in the God's power, the Lord said that none of them would see the 'Promised Land'.

So, we wandered in the wilderness for forty years. Forty testing years.

They moaned about everything. No food - but God fed them. No water – but God always gave them water. It was so hard, I had to go to God so many times to ask for help. Often I had to plead on their part for God not to destroy them.

Even, I did something that displeased God. Looking back, with all the strain and stress – it was no wonder!

The people were moaning again: they wanted water.

God said: "Go to the rock and speak to it and the water will flow."

I was so fed up with the people moaning, I went up to the rock and struck the rock my staff. The water flowed but God was not pleased.

"Did you not believe that I would supply the water? For your disbelief, you will never go into the land I have promised."

There were so many times I had to go to the Lord because the people moaned at me for something. But, mostly they brought things on themselves – like when they turned their back on God and he sent serpents. If a serpent bit them they would die unless they looked upon a bronze serpent God told me to make.

It seemed to happen so many times, the people just kept going their own way. God helped them so many times - and yet they wouldn't listen.

God once used me to help them fight the Amalekites. While I held my rod up high they seemed to be winning - and when I put my arms down the tables turned and they started to lose. Caleb and Hur held up my arms to ensure we won the battle.

We did at last go back to the border of the 'Promised Land' but I was not allowed to go in. God told me to commission Joshua to lead the people and to lead them in to the 'Promised Land.'

After this, I returned to be with God forever.

Story Three

Abraham

My name is Abraham I was born in Ur of the Chaldees. I am the son of Terah. I was called by God to leave his household. So, I left and went to Haran I stayed there twelve years until God called me again.

"Get thee out of thy country to a land I will show you and I will make you a great nation!"

With my flock and herds, I went, taking my nephew Lot and his family with me. I was old, in fact I was 75 years old when I left Haran… but God had promised me I would have a son.

We moved from place to place and the Lord said that he would give all the land that we passed through. While we were camped at Bethel, a famine came on the land so I decided to go down to Egypt.

As I went, I looked at my wife Sarah. She was very beautiful. So, I told the Egyptians that she was my sister. I thought if I said she was my wife they might kill me to get her for themselves. The plan worked for a while and I was treated very well because of her. But God was not happy with me and started to plague the Egyptians.

The Egyptians found out I had lied so they sent me away into the wilderness. While we were there our flocks grew very well. Lot's flocks had grown too and the land was not big enough for us all so we agreed that we should part. I gave Lot the choice: he chose the valley near to Sodom and Gomorra.

Sometime later Lot got captured by the king that conquered Sodom and Gomorra. So I raised up an army from among my servants and went and rescued Lot and Sodom and Gomorra. The king offered to reward me but I declined.

Although God had said we would have a son. I was so old and frail I lost hope. It never seemed to be possible to have a child with Sarah. I gave up waiting and had a son by my wife's servant.

God renewed his promise and said that Sarah my wife would have a baby. I fell on the ground laughing! I was 100 years old and Sarah was 90. But still God said it would happen!

I suggested that Ishmael, the child I had by my wife's servant, could be my heir. But God refused. God then said that all males should be circumcised. By this time Ishmael was thirteen years old.

Then one day two men arrived. I guess they were angels; so, I told my wife to prepare a good meal for them even though they had said not to bother too much. They asked where Sarah was and I replied that she was in the tent. They said she would have a son.

Sarah heard what they said and laughed for she was way past the age to be able to bear a child. God then spoke to me and asked why Sarah laughed. He said: "I will renew her so she shall have a son."

The two men got up. They turned towards Sodom and Gomorra. God told me he was going to destroy them with fire and brimstone. I instantly thought of Lot and his family so I started to plead with God. I said:

"Will you destroy the good with the wicked? Say there are fifty, will you spare them for the sake of fifty?" God said he would spare them for fifty.

"What about forty-five?" I replied. And, God replied saying he would spare them for the sake of forty-five. I kept on pleading for forty then for thirty then for twenty then ten.

The Lord promised he would spare them for forty then thirty then twenty then ten. Then God left me.

The men went down into the city and found Lot and his family. I was told that Lot had to lock the doors because the men of the city tried to get the two angels. In the morning, God blinded the city men so they could not see the angels leave.

Lot's family were told to get out of the city and not look back. But, Lot's wife looked back and so she was turned into a pillar of salt. The cities were destroyed by fire and brimstone. After that we moved too and camped between Kadesh and Shur.

I was once again frightened that because my wife was beautiful they may kill me. So, again I said she was my sister. So, King Abimelech took her to be his wife - but God told him she was my wife. So he sent us away.

Then most amazing thing happened! Sarah became pregnant. What a miracle! Not only were we too old, but God honoured His promise after everything we had done. We had even tried to cheat into getting the end result!

When the child was born we called him Isaac as God had said. It's funny really, God has a sense of humour because Isaac means 'he laughed'. He was a fine lad. He was circumcised on the eighth day. Then, he grew healthy and strong.

Then came a terrible shock. God told me to take him to a mountain and there offer him up as a sacrifice. I felt terrible! But God had said it! So, I had to go…

We took two servants and some wood on a donkey and set of. Isaac asked:

"Where is the animal to sacrifice?" But I just replied, God will provide. I was in a terrible state inside but did not want to show anything was wrong.

When we got near to the place, I told the servants to stay put until we come back. Was I going to be able to do it? Would I be able to kill my son?

We got to the top of the mountain. I picked up some stones built an altar put the wood on it. Then, quickly, I grabbed Isaac and tied him to it. I was screaming inside but I had to obey God!

I pulled out my knife. Rose it up and was about to strike when God shouted: "Stop! Do not harm the boy!"

I quickly untied him and saw a ram caught in a thicket. I took it and made our sacrifice. God was very pleased with me and said it was good that I put His will before my own. I told Isaac what had happened that it was all down to what God had told me to do.

God tested me and I had learned a lesson. God must come first in my life. Not even my son must come before him.

God told me to send Hagar and Ishmael away. So I obeyed. I pleaded with God to bless Ishmael and He agreed to care for him.

Time went by and, when Sarah was 100 years old, she died. I grieved for her but did not know where to bury her. I said to the sons of Heth: "I am a stranger here. Where can I bury my wife?"

I asked them to let me buy some land so I could bury her. So I laid her to rest.

As the years went by, it became time for Isaac to marry I sent my most trusted servant back to our own land to find a bride for Isaac. I told him to ask for God's guidance in everything and he did.

When the servant brought back Rebecca, Isaac loved her as soon as he saw her. So, God had his hand in it all the time. I then took a new wife called Keturah. She bore me Zimran, Jokshan, Medan, Midian, Ishbak and Shuah. As I am telling you this I am 175 and nearing the end of my life. One thing I can tell you is that God honoured His promises.

Story Four

Jacob

I am Jacob. I was born one of twins. I was second to be born. My brother's name was Esau. He was hairy and strong and worked in the field and was a hunter.

My father favoured him because he was strong like a real man. I was pale and fresh of face and favoured my mother not him. When we grew up we knew that he would inherit everything because he was the eldest. It was his birth-right.

One day, I was making some broth when Esau came in and asked for some food.

"I'm starving," he said.

I replied: "In exchange for your birth-right, I will give you food." He was so hungry he agreed. So from that point everything was to come me not him.

The only thing he would inherit was my father's blessing. When the day came, my mother had a plan so that I could get the blessing that should have been Esau's.

She made a broth, rubbed grease on my coat and put hairy skin on my neck and arms so I smelt and felt like Esau.

Since my father was blind, I tricked my father into thinking I was Esau. He blessed me. So, when Esau came for the blessing from his father. He replied that he had already given it. My mother sent me away so Esau could not find me.

She told my father that I had left. I had gone to get a wife from our own people not like Esau who had taken a wife from among the people where we were living.

I travelled as far as I could in one day then had to lie down to sleep. As I slept I had a dream. I saw a ladder reaching from earth to heaven with angels going up and down. My family were at the top.

God renewed the promise to me as he did to my father and my grandfather Abraham. When I awoke, I placed a stone on the spot and anointed it with oil to commemorate the spot where I met God. From that time on I was called Israel.

I travelled on to a well near where our family lived. There I met Rachel. I agreed with her father Laban to work seven years to be able to marry her.

After the seven years, Laban tricked me into marrying her sister Leah. Leah was older so it was customary that she should marry first.

I then had to work another seven years to marry Rachel. As the years went by I had six boys by Leah and a daughter. She gave me her servant Bilhah and I had two sons by her. Then Rachel who we thought was barren gave her me her servant Zilpah, I had two sons by her.

Then came a welcome surprise: Rachel had a son whom I called Joseph. I loved him more than the others because he was the son of the wife I had loved from the beginning.

The time had come for me to return home but Laban tried to trick me to work for a herd of my own to keep myself and my wives. I turned the table on him by telling his sons that he was giving their inheritance away.

So, when he was away from home, we left. He was mad when he found we had gone and came after us. When he eventually caught up with us, we managed to come to an agreement and parted and went our different ways.

When we got near the place where I used to live I got a bit scared of what was going to happen when we met Esau. So, I divided my people and sent messages to Esau. As it happened, when we met there was no trouble at all. We took different parts of the land and we lived in peace.

Shortly after, Rachel got pregnant. Tragedy struck. Even though the baby lived, she died in child birth. We called the baby Benjamin.

I was torn in two. She was the one I had loved from the beginning! I had to carry on because I had a big family to look after. I got Joseph a special coat because he was my favourite son.

Then something odd happened. Joseph had dreams which showed that we would all one day bow down to him. I told him to be careful because as you can imagine, his brothers did not like it. Joseph also told me if they did things wrong.

Then, one day, his brothers were out with the herd and had been away a long time. I sent him with some food and told him to come back and tell me if they were alright. Well, he was away a long time then they all came back without him with his coat covered in blood.

They told me that he must have been killed by a wild animal. This was terrible! First my favourite wife and now my favourite son! This was the end of Joseph or so I thought.

Well, over the next seven years we had good crops. The crops were brilliant! We were really having an abundance of crops. Everything was going well.

Then the tide seemed to turn. Everything seemed to go wrong. It didn't rain on the crops and so there was no water. The crops would not grow. We were starving.

We were getting desperate. We heard that there was plenty of food in Egypt. So, I sent ten of my sons to Egypt. I kept the youngest of Rachel's sons at home. He was the one thing that reminded me of her.

They went and they were gone a long time. When they got back Simeon was missing. They said the man in Egypt said they were spies.

"He said he would keep Simeon there until we went again. Strangely, we have to take Benjamin next time," my sons said.

The food was good but we had a shock. The money we paid had been put back in their sacks.

We agreed that we would take it all back next time they went. So, the day came they had to go back and they took Benjamin with them. I was not happy but we had no choice.

It seemed a long time. Longer than the first time they had gone. When they got back, I could not believe my ears.

They said that Joseph was in charge of all of Egypt and we were all to move to Egypt so he could look after us. I did not believe them at first but he had sent carts and chariots to take us there.

It was a long journey. But, when I saw Joseph my heart nearly burst with joy. All of his dreams had come true and through it he saved us. I now could die a happy man.

Story Five

David

I am David, the youngest son of Jesse of Bethlehem. I have seven brothers but they had a different mother to me and they were not keen on me at all so I was sent out to look after the sheep.

I spent a lot of my time singing and talking to God. Life was not always easy because there were wild animals there. I even had to kill a bear! Another time I killed a lion! You may wonder about how well I could kill a lion with my sling... or a bear with one accurate stone! The stone would smash into their skull. But you had to make sure you did not miss.

I was happy. Nobody seemed to bother me. Then one day one of my father's servants came and said:

"You have to come down to the house. Samuel the prophet has come and wants to see you."

"Me?!" I said, "What for?"

"I don't know just come," came the reply.

When I arrived, Samuel the priest was waiting eagerly. He said:

"This is the one!" He then told me to kneel so I did and he anointed me with oil. Then he went away, I went back to my sheep. A confusing event in anyone's mind!

Sometime later, my father called me and said:

"I have some food here for your brothers who are fighting in the army. Take it to them."

So, off I went but when I arrived nobody was fighting. I was completely baffled. I thought: "What is going on!"

Then I heard a man from the other side of the valley shout. It was a loud shout.

"Come out and fight our champion! If you win, we will be your slaves if we win then you will be ours!"

Nobody moved. Not an inch! I asked to a soldier next to me:

"Isn't there anybody willing to fight him?"

"He's too big," was the reply.

My brothers saw me and asked me what I was doing here. They accused me of coming to spy on them.

"No, I brought you some food!"

They took the food and said go home. Before I left, I said to the soldiers around me:

"We have God on our side!"

"Well you go and fight him then!" they laughed!

"I will," I said and they looked dumbfounded. Some soldiers took me to the king and said that I was ready to fight Goliath. The king got up out of his throne and put his armour on me. It was no good… it was so heavy that I could not walk. I took it off and said to the king:

"God will fight for me today."

So, I started down the valley. I picked five good stones and got my sling ready. They had told Goliath I was coming. He loomed out over the horizon. He stood up. I had never seen such a giant! He made fun of me saying:

"They have sent a boy with sticks and stones to kill me! I will cut you up and feed you to the birds."

I said: "I will chop off your head!"

He laughed at me and when I got near enough I put a stone in my sling. I swung it round and round and round... then let it fly! It hit him right on the forehead! It smashed into his head and he fell to the ground!

I ran up... he was dead! I picked up his own sword and chopped off his head and held it up so the whole army could see! Then the army rose up and the enemy ran for their lives. Our army chased them right back to their own city.

* * *

After killing Goliath, Saul the king would not let me go home. I became a soldier and soon after he put me in charge of the army. We went out and defeated our enemies. God was on our side! And, of course, it made me very popular with the crowds that welcomed us back, so much so that the women in the street started to shout:

"Saul has killed his thousands, but David has killed his tens of thousands."

This upset the king and he sent men many times to try to kill me. He threw a javelin at me!

When I killed Goliath, he promised me his daughter in marriage but she went and married someone else. This was so unfair! He had another daughter who loved me. So, when I asked if I could marry her, he told me I had to kill 200 Philistines. He, of course, said this hoping I would get killed!

But God was on my side.

I also had someone who always told me what sort of mood the king was in and if it was safe to go into the palace. I went there very often to play my harp for the king to calm him down.

Jonathan and I were very good friends and there were many times when he saved my life from his father. We made lots of signals so that he could let me know when it was safe to go near the palace.

The last signal, before I went away, was that he went out to practice his arrow shooting. If he told the boy go further on to get the arrow, then it was not safe for me to return.

So I left and tried to get into a Philistine city by trying to act as if I was mad. But, then, I decided to hide in some caves. Soon I was joined by a lot of men who had at sometime or another fallen out with King Saul.

Although we were strong, we did nothing against Saul or our people because he was the God anointed one.

Twice I had a chance to kill him. Once, I even, cut off the hem of his garment. Another time, I took his spear from by his head with his cup. Both times he said he would not come after me… but he did.

I then went to live with the Philistines. Until one day, when I had just returned from fighting the Amalekites, a man arrived with all his clothes torn. He told me that he had escaped from a battle. At that battle, he saw Saul in a hopeless position. Saul had asked him to kill him. So he did.

In anger, I said: "Who gave you the right to kill the Lord's anointed!"

I then had him killed. Jonathan had died in the same battle. I went in to a time of deep morning.

After a while, I was asked up to a town where they proclaimed me King. Gradually, I became king of all Israel because God blessed me in all I tried to do.

I always asked Him if I was to go into battle or not. I was blessed by God and was able to write many psalms and songs to praise Him.

Just as all things seemed to be going well. I just couldn't help myself. I did a bad thing, I saw my neighbour's wife bathing and I wanted her.

I took her to my bed because I wanted to keep her. I arranged for my neighbour to fight in the front line of a battle so that he would be killed. This is exactly what happened.

I thought I had got away with it because nothing seemed to happen. That was until Nathan the prophet came to the palace and told a story of a man who had done wrong.

I replied to Nathan's story and said the man was bad and should die because of his sins.

In a surprise turn of events, he muttered: "The bad one is you!"

I was found out and God made me pay. Things did not always go right: my one son killed his brother. I should have put him to death! But I just couldn't! I banned him from the country and yet while he was away he tried to start a revolution against me!

But you see God was still on my side. On his way coming to get me, my son's hair got caught in a tree. He was then killed by Joab.

After his death, that grieved me very much, I no longer went out to do battle myself. I had another son by Bathsheba and called him Solomon and he was to be my heir to the throne.

I had a passion, I had a longing to do something. I wanted to build a temple to the Lord. But that was not to be. God said that there was too much blood on my hands. And so the temple would be built by my son, Solomon. And that's how it all came to end...

13649639R00024

Printed in Great Britain
by Amazon.co.uk, Ltd.,
Marston Gate.